The Moon Telegrams
Volume One

January 2021-June 2021

Annaliese Morgan

First published in the UK by Black Daisy Press
49 Greek Street London W1D 4EG

www.blackdaisypress.com

© Annaliese Morgan 2021
The right of Annaliese Morgan to be identified as the author of this work has been asserted by her in accordance with the Copyright, Designs and Patents Act 1988.

All Rights Reserved.

No part of this book may be printed, reproduced or utilised in any form or by any electronic, mechanical or other means, now known or hereafter invented, including photocopying and recording, or in any information storage retrieval system, without permission in writing from the publishers.

This is a work of non-fiction, and the author has made every effort to provide accurate information and credits. Any inaccuracies or missing information will be resolved in subsequent reprints upon notification. Neither the author nor publisher is responsible for results accrued from any advice given in this book as it may not be suitable for every situation.

A catalogue record for this book is available from the British Library

Printed and bound in the UK

ISBN: 978-1-8384163-3-1

*Dedicated to all those who ever
wondered about life.*

Annaliese Morgan is an English author, inspirational role model and expert in the supernatural and mystical realms. Originally from Yorkshire but lives in London with her two sons, a basset hound called Pineapple and too many books. Her writing career began way back in the late nineties and includes both non-fiction and fiction. Annaliese primarily writes in the genres of supernatural, fantasy and contemporary and she has been featured on BBC Radio, Stage 32, Woman Magazine, Woman's Own Magazine, Stylist and many others. Annaliese and her two boys (The M's or the three musketeers as they are referred too) are also avid travellers and a creative family doing life their own way.

You can find out more about Annaliese, her work or sign up for her newsletter at

www.annaliesemorgan.com

Previous Titles by Annaliese Morgan

Breaking Chains – autobiographical inspiring vignettes

Desperate Housepets – Become a chic pet owner without being a bitch

How to get through NVQ 2 veterinary Nurses

How to get through NVQ 3 veterinary Nurses

A-Z for veterinary nurses

Anaesthesia and analgesia chapter in BSAVA Manual for Veterinary Nurses

Forthcoming Titles by Annaliese Morgan

Stay Wild

Rocked by Love

The Moon Telegrams Volume Two

Contents

January 2021 – Supernatural guidance	1
February 2021 – Tree symbology	8
March 2021 – Mermaids and sirens	16
April 2021 – Ancient Egyptian magic	23
May 2021 – Energy fields and auras	30
June 2021 – Spirit Guides and Keys	37
Contact the Author	43
Bibliography	44

Introduction

At the end of 2020 I decided to create The Moon telegrams; free digital vintage looking vignettes delivered to subscribers every month on the day of the new moon. Each telegram interprets and explains interesting themes and subjects about the supernatural world, mythical beings, the Cosmos and ancient secrets. They are non-fiction, informative and open the mind to other realities and possibilities, or it might just twist it a little, as you start to ask bigger *why* questions about life and probe further into what is true and what isn't within our human existence.

They became more popular than I first anticipated and little treasures one can keep. It bothered me these pieces of work would eventually become lost in the slush of email bins, so I wrote and created extended versions of each monthly telegram to make them into volumes. These volumes will be published every six months. The Moon Telegrams are the new (cooler) collectible comics!

You will find explanations on supernatural entities, mermaids, vampires, symbology, energies of the Cosmos, dragons, psychic abilities, ancient secrets that have been disguised for hundreds of years and so much more.

The point of The Moon Telegrams is to expand and enrich your life. To introduce you to your own mystical journey, ignite an unlit match within you or deepen your knowledge on which already interests you. Each of these telegrams are books and subject matter in their own right so please know there is far more behind each telegram you can investigate, and I invite you to do so. The information in these telegrams can often be incorporated into *your way of being and life* too, aiding you to live how you wish to.

The Moon Telegrams are timeless and ageless and will apply at whatever stage or year you are reading these. You may read them all in one sitting, dip in and out or refer back to them whenever you want or need to.

I have studied for decades on all these topics and areas of the supernatural, the mystical and esoteric thought. I am qualified in diplomas in many of these subjects (including vampirology, symbology, ancient Egyptian magic and dragons) and I have trained with the country's best psychics and mediums. For years, and still today, I am repeatedly asked for advice or sought out to answer questions about life and the unseen realms... I guarantee you have asked yourself questions about not only the meaning of your life but what else is going on, is there really a supernatural world and something bigger than I?

My answer is a resounding yes.

I hope I move you into an enchanting life,

Annaliese.

The Moon Telegrams

Date: January 13th, 2021
England

Welcome to the first new moon and first Moon Telegram of 2021.

Given we all deserve a stellar year, I wanted to send a telegram on how we receive intuition and supernatural (psychic) guidance, which can change your life dramatically.

Far from being woo woo or fortune telling from a lady in a caravan with a pink neon sign, psychic guidance is something we all have access to, and it can change your life. It can save your life. It can assist you in achieving success, love, peace, direction and living a life beyond your wildest dreams. If you wish to be ahead of the game and more confident and trusting of yourself, you will find this information invaluable. At certain times in our life convergence with the higher realms of the Cosmos may be all we have, and in truth, it will deliver every time if you learn how to attune to it and interpret the information.

We are not rattling about alone on planet earth left to our own devices, we have a personal support team in the Cosmos to which we are connected to by intuition and psychic portals. A hunch *we feel, or sense* is no different to receiving information from someone in an email or letter, they are just communicated and received in different frequencies. Except the former is substantially more powerful, significant, simpler and ahead of time.

Intuition and psychic guidance are different but with elements that are closely linked. Intuition is perhaps more widely accepted and acknowledged, both intuition and supernatural guidance have the common trait of giving you inspired hunches, which I dare say you are already familiar with. Inspired hunches move us to inspired action (not motivated action), which moves us to our goal or intentions. Inspired action is superior to forcing or figuring out things on your own strength alone. Motivation, on the other hand, is what you need when you lack the necessary connections with yourself and struggle to believe in your abilities.

Inspiration means to be 'in spirit,' to be 'in alignment' with the energies of the Cosmos, your higher self and your Guides. They know more than we do and have a view from the mountain top, as opposed to the view we have stood in the valley.

The energies of the higher realms are unable to talk to us like we do with people, they communicate via intuition, symbols, and psychic guidance. It will serve you well to learn how we receive intuition, messages from the Cosmos and psychic guidance so you can utilise it better in your life.

Everyone is different, and each will have their own way of receiving, recognising and interpreting. You may begin to realise you have been doing this already but unknowingly. Either way, have fun and spend time learning your own combination of skills. It is only the experiences which will teach you and enable you to master these skills.

Where does intuition (gut feeling, hunches, sixth sense) come from?

Intuition is a hit of insight, foresight, a knowing about something or someone you can't explain it but just sense or know... remember, energy never lies. People and their words might but their energy doesn't and can't.

Intuition comes partially from reams and reams of information stored in the subconscious brain from all the different lifetimes we have lived. It is also tied to two of the portals in which we receive psychic guidance. Intuition tends to come more naturally to females than males, but both are equally capable. Both male and females have a mixture of feminine and masculine energy with one usually more dominate and hence the two the genders. For females, and those who identify as being or having a more predominate female energy, need to realise the power of the female energy and intuition. How they can achieve far more by sitting in this energy and operating from this divine feminine place rather than from the hustle, motivated, 'doing' energy of the masculine. Neither is wrong unless you are constantly trying to do life from the wrong energy foundation for you. We will delve into this topic in a later telegram.

As you become more well versed in intuition, you will find you naturally take intuitive (inspired) action without thinking. You will recognise and trust those hunches quicker, clearer and more profoundly. The more you take note and acknowledge when you 'were right' the stronger your intuition becomes.

Psychics and Mediums

The difference? As a psychic you receive information from your Higher Self, your Guides and the Cosmos (God, Spirit, Allah, The Universe, Love... whatever name is on the door for you) and you can interpret (read) the energy of other human beings who are alive.

Mediums do all of this too plus they can converse with those who have passed away and over to the spirit realm. Every medium is a psychic but not every psychic is a medium. Mediums at one time used to be known as clairvoyants. This is no longer the case as clairvoyance is actually a skill and a portal in which we download or receive information as psychic guidance.

BUT I'M NOT A PSYCHIC?

Oh, but you are! You may not be a medium, but all humans are psychic. It is how well you develop and practice the skills which determines your abilities.

How do we receive or download psychic guidance and information?

There are four main portals (ways) in which information is received, with two of these usually stronger than the others and therefore we are 'better at' those skills. These can swap about allowing the other portals to become more developed but all four are available to us at all times.

It is important to be in a calm, centred state. Psychic guidance comes in through stillness and silence not through chaos, stress and scatteredness. It is subtle, particularly at first, not always logical but the more you practice the more sense it makes to you.

Clairvoyance – 'Clear Seeing.' Often known as the third eye or mind's eye. A person with this skill will, in their head, see images, scenes, colours, and symbols. Anything visual. This is open to interpretation and why practice is important to correctly translate the meaning of the symbolic images you are given, which will be personal to you. It plays out like a screen on the inside of your forehead. Some with this skill see orbs and spirit forms in normal waking life.

Clairaudience – 'Clear Hearing.' A person with this skill can hear voices, whispers, singing or sounds in general. It can sound like your own voice, an inner voice or the voice of a Guide or Spirit. The latter tends to be disjointed and difficult to understand as they have to lower their vibration in order for you to hear them. Clairaudience can also be received as ideas, thoughts or a block of thought you unravel naturally, commonly through speech.

Clairsentience – 'Clear feeling.' A person with this skill feels emotions in their body. These are either of another person or from your supernatural team in the Cosmos. Healers use this to detect problem areas. It is also a great skill to use to underpin the other skills when interpreting. Example, you see an image of suitcase being packed which could mean many things, but how does it *feel*, in your body? The solar plexus area (upper abdomen) is a common area to sense emotions and feelings. Intuition is intertwined with Clairsentience.

Claircognizance – 'Clear Knowing.' A person with this skill just knows things! They will know information or have a fully formed idea without understanding how. They are naturally wise, and people gravitate towards you for advice... as you always seem to know what to say or do. Again, intuition is intertwined with Claircognizance.

There are another two portals some people experience but these two are much rarer:

Clairalience – 'Clear smell.' They receive guidance through smells given to them and can smell the particular scent in the air around them.

Clairgustance – 'Clear taste.' They are given guidance through different tastes, again this person can taste these flavours in their mouth.

OTHER WAYS GUIDANCE OR SIGNS ARE COMMUNICATED

Your supernatural team will always meet you where you are at and communicate in ways you can notice and understand. Here are some more to look out for, as the Cosmos will use a plethora of ways and platforms, in order for us to receive the right message at the right time in a way that is meaningful.

- Through journaling or free writing
- Talking out loud to yourself or to the Cosmos
- Via songs, books, articles, TV shows or films
- Through other people and conversations, these act as messengers on behalf of the Cosmos
- Through meditation
- Social media posts
- Advertisements
- Phone calls and text messages
- Symbols and numbers, particularly if they are repeated or noted in an unusual setting
- Birds – birds are excellent carriers of messages and meanings. Often, they punctate a correct thought or idea at the time by showing up or behaving unusually
- The animal kingdom – animals are important messengers. Each carry a universal meaning and likely further messages or information personal to you. There is plenty information online and in books to research this further and I highly recommend it.

You will know if it is a message, sign or guidance from the Cosmos because it will either feel like sudden relief or it will make you gasp and look twice almost blindsiding you a little. Note, signs show up when you are not looking for them. Don't try to make them fit your desired outcome either! No sign (after asking) is also a message i.e., it's a no and time to redirect.

WILL I SEE A GHOST?

This is something a lot of people fear and shouldn't. Ignore the portrayal of ghosts in movies and TV shows! The truth is, it takes a lot of energy (too much) for a spirit to appear as an earthly ghost to the human eye and so they rarely do it. Especially because they have so many other means of communicating. It does happen but it is extremely rare. Even the most trusted mediums and talented psychics in the world don't experience this.

If you are clairvoyant you may see orbs, strips or flashes of gold and other coloured lights from either those who have passed, Spirit itself, Angels or your Guides.

Document all findings, information received, and signs noticed. You will begin to see patterns, guidance and answers. We think we will remember but more likely we do not and quite often the guidance is something you witness in reality later on. It can be quite mind blowing when you look through and read back through all the information you have documented.

Do have fun with receiving supernatural guidance and discovering your abilities! Research the topic further as this information here is all but the opening into this topic.

The next telegram arrives February 11th, 2021.

The Moon Telegrams

Date: February 11th, 2021
England

Hello to one and all,

As most of the world is in some sort of lockdown or restrictions, I wanted to send a telegram regarding symbology. More specifically on one symbol you can look too, if for no other reason than to enjoy the outdoors and spark interest during these rather dull times. It's difficult to choose just one to discuss, as symbology is a vast subject.

Symbols and their secret complex meanings are hidden in plain sight everywhere and provide us mortals with guidance, knowledge and information constantly if you know how to spot them and interpret their meaning.

I finally landed on revealing a majestic part of nature and its ancient symbolic meanings and it's one you most likely see daily. There are also fun tasks for you at the end.

Trees

Not only do trees stand with beauty and opulence whilst helping to sustain our planet, but they hold tremendous symbolic meaning and wisdom in many cultures. There is deeper meaning to each species of tree and to all its parts as you will come to understand, and in much of folklore, trees are homes to fairies and spirits.

Trees themselves represent life, wisdom, power and prosperity. Each part of the tree also holds a meaning. Consider this the next time you come across one of its parts (especially if it's in an unusual way or setting), it could be helping you or reflecting a part of you which needs attention, or part of you haven't acknowledged.

Tree roots represent depth, support and solid foundations
Tree trunks represent strength, reliability and masculine energy
Tree branches represent reach, growth, protection and feminine energy
The leaves represent warmth and softness
The fruits represent energy, food and nourishment
Seeds represent future ideas, knowledge, information and the release of it

Let's drop right into Celtic symbology... The Moon Month Calendar and its tree symbology. There are thirteen moon months a year, each associated with a tree of significance. As a side note the word *month* comes from the word moon.

1st Moon Month. December 24th – January 21st. The Birch Tree
Symbolising birth, purification and fertility. It represents looking ahead, contemplation and the feminine energy. The birch tree is known as The Lady of the Woods.

2nd Moon Month. January 22nd – February 17th. The Rowan Tree
Symbolising healing, protection, guardianship and supports psychic (supernatural) energies. It's berries,

interestingly, hold a pentagram shape suggesting powerful forces.

3rd Moon Month. February 18th – March 17th. The Ash Tree

The Ash Tree is a sacred tree to Druids. It Symbolises higher awareness, magical and potent healing. It's also used in many fantasy and supernatural stories.

4th Moon Month. March 18th – April 14th. The Alder Tree

Symbolises protection, getting in tune with your intuitive abilities, making decisions.

5th Moon Month. April 15th – May 12th. The Willow Tree

The Willow tree planted near the home wards away danger. It symbolises, the moon, women and mysteries, wishing, healing, growth, protection and fertility.

6th Moon Month. May13th – June9th. The Hawthorn Tree

Symbolises balance, masculine energy and fire, fertility and harmonious relationships.

7th Moon Month. June 10th – July 7th. The Oak Tree

The Oak Tree is also sacred to Druids. It symbolises success, money, good fortune, strength and stability. Its acorns are associated with new beginnings.

8th Moon Month. July 8th – August 4th. The Holly Tree

Symbolises masculine energy, firmness, protection, overcoming anger, power and leadership.

9th Moon Month. August 5th – September 1st. The Hazel Tree
'The life force within you.' Symbolises divination, wisdom and inspiration. Tapping into the well of knowledge and intuition within.

10th Moon Month. September 2nd – September 29th. The Vine Tree
Symbolises bounty, opportunity and regeneration. The great harvest, happiness and wrath i.e., passionate emotions.

11th Moon Month. September 30th - October 27th. Ivy
Symbolises binding, tenacity, but can also be smothering and struggle. Ivy often continues to live even when its host plant has died... representing 'life goes on' and the cycle of life-death-rebirth.

12th Moon Month. October 28th – November 23rd. The Reed Tree
Symbolises communication., divination, purification and clarification.

13th Moon Month. November 24th – December 23rd. The Elder Tree
Symbolises endings and beginnings. Purging of the unwanted, birth and death. The Elder Tree is damaged easily but also springs back to life easily hence it leads us into the new year.

For Harry Potter fans, you may notice (now) how many of the wands used were made from the wood of these particular trees.

Birth Month Trees

The Celtic druids also believed your birth date is linked to The Moon Month Calendar and the formation of your personality. They developed The Celtic Tree Astrology system. As it is linked to The Moon Calendar month there are thirteen astrological signs instead of twelve. Trees are distinctly important to the Celtics. Their knowledge of them and of the earth's cycles is profound.

December 24th – January 21st. The Birch Tree
Natural leader with high energy, ambition, tolerance and tough. You can become caught up in your zest and drive, but you motivate others well. You brighten up rooms and others with your charm and quick wit.

January 22nd – February 17th. The Rowan Tree
You are a visionary with high ideals. Definitely a thinker, you are also influential but in a subtle way. You burn bright with inner passion which does get you noticed but your originality and creativity can be misunderstood by others. Sometimes you can be aloof.

February 18th – March 17th. The Ash Tree
Always in touch with your inner muse, intuition and imagination you are a free thinker, artistic and inspired by nature. You inspire others but can be reclusive and moody at times. You disregard what others think of you and constantly reinvent.

March 18th – April 14th. The Alder Tree
Trailblazers and pathfinders. Full of charm and a circulator you have strong faith in yourself with a distaste for waste and fake people or superficial feelings. People love to follow you and you mix well because your self-assurance is infectious to others.

April 15th – May 12th. The Willow Tree
You are an observer, ruled by the moon and mystical. Naturally creative, intelligent and intuitive you understand cycles and seasons and tend to be patient. Your ability to retain and offer information impresses others. You are full of potential but can hold yourself back for fear of appearing too much.

May 13th – June 9th. The Hawthorn Tree
There are two sides to you; on the inner you are a creative fire, full of passion and are romantic but externally appear to others as 'normal' and more average. You don't give yourself enough credit at times but are a great listener, curious and great at adapting to change. You are somewhat of an illusionist.

June 10th – July 7th. The Oak Tree
Your gift is strength. You champion and crusade for those without a voice or the underdog. Generous, nurturing and helpful you ooze confidence and believe in positive outcomes. You may be a teacher as you love to offer your knowledge and have a passion for history and ancestry. You enjoy large families or large social settings.

July 8th – August 4th. The Holly Tree
Regal, noble and high minded, you are happy to take on positions of high status, power and be a leader. You overcome challenges with your rare skills and remain focused on outcomes. Rarely defeated as you always keep going. Confidence in your abilities can be mistaken for arrogance but once others get to know you, you are warm, generous and helpful.

August 5th – September 1st. The Hazel Tree
Gifted in academia, you are a knower, intelligent and efficient. You retain information well and dazzle others with this. You have an eye for detail but can be controlling and prefer to make rules rather than follow them.

September 2nd – September 29th. The Vine Tree
You can be unpredictable and indecisive because you see both sides and the good of each in a story or situation. You have the Midas touch and like the finer things in life. Despite being aloof at times you are super romantic. Your charm, elegance and esteem attract a large following.

September 30th - October 27th. Ivy
You have an ability to overcome all odds and are a survivor yet sometimes feel life is unfair to you. You are giving, helpful, compassionate and loyal filled with charm, charisma and a deep-rooted faith. Your great wit and intellect is a winner.

October 28th – November 23rd. The Reed Tree
A true keeper of secrets and you delve in to find the real truth of things. Yet you do love stories, gossip, scandal and lore. You may be a journalist, a historian, or archaeologist. You love people and are a great networker with strong honour.

November 24th – December 23rd. The Elder Tree
A freedom loving wild child and seeker. You may live life in the fast lane and although you are more extrovert you can be withdrawn. Deeply thoughtful, considerate and helpful you need constant challenges to occupy your mind and body.

FUN TASKS

- Look outside your home, on your street, place of work or other important places to you. Are any of these significant trees there? What could it be telling you? Ask yourself why you live there. Or why are you moving *from* or *to* there. Is there a reason you work at your specific location? Consider the hidden meaning of the trees around you or those around you in your past.
- Find your ideal match! The Celtics will predict your best astrological matches according to tree sign combability and their tree zodiac. Research this topic.
- Hug a tree! Or place your hands for 30 seconds or longer on their trunk. In silence and with closed eyes, feel its wisdom and magic. Any tree will do but you can choose one from the above list and begin to tap into their specific qualities. You will feel their energy, and it's incredibly grounding, healing and informative.

The next telegram will arrive March 13th, 2021.

The Moon Telegrams

Date: March 13th, 2021
England

Hello to one and all,

I wanted to send a telegram this month to enrich our lives and lift our spirits, and who better to call upon to do this than mermaids?

For thousands of years delightful mermaids and other mythical creatures of Earths' waters have captured our imaginations and interests. The word mermaid comes from the old English word 'Mere' (meaning sea) and 'maid' (meaning young girl/woman). Other beauties of the waters include sirens, selkies, sprites and nymphs. In later telegrams there will be more on the sexy sirens, selkie's, sprites and nymphs although there is a peek into those included here.

Origins of Mermaids

There are multiple theories and stories relating to how mermaids came to be. Most continents and countries have their own well documented tales, with a general agreement that these magical half human/half fish entities, have existed for thousands and thousands of years.

The first recorded mermaid was in 1000 BC. Her name was Atargatis from Syria. A Goddess who threw herself in a lake to become a fish due to (according to legend) her own disgrace and shame at accidentally killing her human love interest. The water would not allow Atargatis to relinquish her beauty and become a fish, so it transformed her into a mermaid instead. Ancient Temples, coins and other items have been found with Atargatis represented on them.

Hans Christian Anderson's, The Little Mermaid (a fairy tale he wrote in 1836,) is perhaps one of the most famous mermaids and the statue of The Little Mermaid in Copenhagen, Denmark is an iconic global tourist attraction.

The first representation of a mermaid in England can be found in Durham Castle. It was built in 1078, the carving also shows the mermaid in a hunting scene with two leopards. Churches in early years used the symbol of the mermaid as a way to remind their following that vanity (a trait closely associated with mermaids) is one of the seven deadly sins. Mermaids are carved in stone upon many sacred structures such as The Notre Dame in France and St. Lawrence in England.

WHERE DO MERMAIDS LIVE?

Mermaids, merman (merfolk), and sirens live in many kinds of water not just the ocean. These creatures inhabit rivers, waterfalls, lakes, fountains and wells. In our modern times mermaids can happily live on land for days, weeks or months, although the water is their *home,* to which they will invariably return to. It is thought their abodes can include places like coral caves and the sunken city of lost Atlantis at the bottom of the ocean.

MERMAID QUALITIES

Mermaids are alluring, strong, glamorous, magical, seductive, fun and lucky. They are benevolent powerful creatures many a human man falls in love with, and human women admire. Equally, mermaids can cause havoc, be dangerous and mischievous. This duality of light and dark has been compared with that of human women. It is also noteworthy the ocean (or water in general) represents the feminine, the subconscious and our emotions. With all this combined it is thought these similarities of mermaids and women is a root cause of our fascination with them.

Mermaids delve down deep in the waters, riding the waves and dig up gifts and treasures from the bottom of the ocean floor to give to us all, as well as themselves. The human subconscious mind drives most of our actions, running our own show on autopilot. Until we delve into our murky minds and life, bringing the dark into the light, initiating healing and a new improved way of operating. Can you connect the correlation to the mermaids?

Whether we are male or female, mermaids encourage us to do this work. To feel the connection with our true selves, to find our own opulence and beauty and to portray ourselves unapologetically.

Dazzling abilities of mermaids and their weaknesses

They are physically stunning creatures with eternal youth, pearly skin, bright eyes and coral lips but they are also vain. Sitting on rocks combing their hair, admiring their appearance and fanning their fish tails is a common past time.

- They have a distinct and beautiful singing voice. Captivating, if not hypnotising, humans worldwide.
- They can offer humans protection and also give them

the ability to breath under water if they wish too... should they find a friend in a human or human they have fallen in love with for example.
- Mermaids will always help those who helped them, but woe betide anyone who crosses them.
- Mermaids are able to breathe underwater, dive to depths no human can and are able to survive in deep waters, hence why many can live out in the ocean. Reaching speeds of up to 600Km/h you would be hard pressed to catch one.
- They possess superhuman strength with their tails being the most powerful. Their tails can transform into legs making them human so they may live and interact on land. Mermaids are curious creatures and will shed their (up to two meters long) tail to investigate land life and humans.
- Living up to 300 years, they hold the power of fate to decide whether sailors or humans live or die. The weather is a mirror reflection of their emotions and they can create wild hurricanes or calm. They have the ability to manipulate the weather and water, they can boil water, freeze it and make a jelly type substance from it also. Was it a storm, or was a mermaid angry?
- Often depicted as vain creatures with a mirror sat on the rocks admiring their appearance and brushing their hair (interestingly *hair* is a symbol of a female's power), the mirror is not only for their vanity. It's a tool for clairvoyance, allowing mermaids to see into the future. Perhaps representative of our own psychic skills as noted in January's Moon Telegram.
- Telepathy – this is how mermaids, mermen and sirens communicate with each other.
- Dehydration, fire and the sun can damage

mermaids, causing them to burn up if they are exposed to it for too long.
* Their sonic hearing can work against them as artificial sonar used by humans is too strong and knocks them out clean.

Mermaid related watering (and coffee) holes

The Mermaid Tavern, London, England

In the Elizabethan period a tavern existed in Cheapside, London. Its entrance was situated on Bread Street. Today the old entrance can be found between Bread Street and Cannon Street. It is here, on every first Friday of the month, a group of literary Elizabethan gentlemen would meet and drink jovially. The group included names such as: John Donne, Thomas Coryat, Ben Johnson John Seldon and some believe William Shakespeare, although Shakespeare being part of this group is debatable. The building was unfortunately destroyed in 1666 in The Great Fire of London.

Starbucks

Another symbolic representation of the mermaid is seen on the logo of Starbucks. The green lady with two funny looking arms stems from the very early mermaids.

Mermaids' tails used to be split into two, rather than being a solid one-piece tail we are all familiar with. Starbucks use this symbol to reflect the qualities of mermaids in their work and mission... to be inviting and enticing and emit allure, beauty and fun.

The two tailed mermaids also indicate mermaids could interact with humans and partake in love making.

SIRENS

Sirens are a darker temptress, and over time have largely been replaced by mermaids alone. Originally in Greek mythology, sirens were half human and half bird. It was only upon the rise of Christianity they lost their wings and talons and gained a fish tail. Sirens sing a beautiful song from down within the ocean. It spellbinds sailors who then either crash their ships or dive overboard to find the enchanting female; drowning in the process by default or by the siren, who then feasts upon the sailor. Sailors are warned to stay away from such sightings and songs at sea. Mermaids, incidentally, also sing and enchant sailors but do not kill and eat them like their darker ancestors.

SELKIES

Selkies are mythical beings, seals that shapeshift by shedding their skins and becoming human. They are an Irish and Scottish legend. Seen upon Scottish, Irish and English beaches these selkies are as pretty and as alluring as mermaids but must hide their skins safely when they come ashore, otherwise they cannot return to their home of the water. Selkies are predominately female, although there a few seductive male Selkies about too. Both may remain on land as humans and have families. Some families claim to have descended from Selkies such as the MacPhee/MacFie Scottish clans. A famous folklore story in Scotland states a man discovered a naked female selkie on a shore and made her his wife. He stole her skin and throughout their marriage, according to the story, she could be found by the ocean staring out at it, longing for home.

Many sightings and recordings of these magical and

inspiring creatures (particularly mermaids and selkies) have been documented for thousands of years and still are today. Decide for yourself on the authenticity and truth of these but with 97% of the earth's oceans unexplored, and given they can live at depths we can't reach and live as humans; can you be 100% life betting certain that mermaids and ocean folk don't exist?

I think we all can take on a few aspects of the mermaid qualities into our lives, if not the symbology of what mermaids so complexly represent.

Happy frolicking and oceanic empowerment.

The next telegram will arrive on 12th April 2021.

The Moon Telegrams

Date: April 12th, 2021
England

Hello to one and all,

As we all fumble our way out of Covid into a welcomed renaissance, right about now would be a good time to bring in magic.

'Magic' is a broad term and has various names. It is documented, understood and used in multiple ways. All ancient texts, all religious texts, from witches to philosophers to the ancient Egyptians are essentially saying the same thing however, there is a mystical power greater than humans. A supernatural force residing in the Cosmos and within each of us available for our discovery, and for us to use to co create the life we desire.

Ancient Egyptians and their magic are a gripping rabbit hole of a topic because the concrete evidence of their presence and work cannot be denied. The significance of their ancient architecture, like The Pyramids and The Sphinx, and how they deliberately line up with the astronomy of the sky above them and other parts of earth's anatomy like equators, is enough to boggle our reptilian minds alone. How did they do this, know this, and what were they trying to tell us? Something to ponder in a later telegram. As for this new moon, we are delving into Ancient Egyptian Magic.

Magic was part of everyday life in ancient Egypt, it wasn't a case of 'do we believe or not believe' they just did. It was a given; like we view gravity. All believed but it was The Magicians who would perform spells, healings and rituals to bring about the desired result for any visiting individual. Magic was used across the board whether male or female, rich or poor, religious or not.

The difference between religion and magic is this: in religion, it is a God who accesses (prays) to supernatural powers to bring about–or not–the outcome you ask for. There is not always an end goal in religion as you are placing your request at the hands of the deity. It is the God or deity who decides whether you receive your outcome or not.

In magic there is always an end goal. The outcome is specific, but it is The Magician who accesses the supernatural forces and uses them to bring about the outcome or goal requested. It is believed to be *certain* rather than a 'will I be granted this blessing or not?'

Magicians would be sought out by individuals and asked to help them achieve a certain goal, a healing, interpret a dream, or help to develop a higher understanding of supernatural and spiritual worlds. They used spells, wands, amulets, potions, incense and rituals amongst other secretive ways to do their work.

THE MAGICIANS

In brief there were two types of Magicians, and they were trained in secret, in secret places.

Priest-Magicians – These were trained in temples and usually ran their own temple.

Lay Magicians – These were not associated with any organisation or temple.

Priest Magicians were the more common of the two and they had duties to do as part of their role. Although classified as Priests, in ancient Egypt a Priest did not constitute a man or woman of the Holy cloth as one would assume. A Priest or Priestess was a position and status. They would work in the community from which they made their living.

Both males and females practiced Priest/Priestess and magical duties and the majority of Magicians would have a toolbox containing their necessary items, examples include wands, quills, seeds and small statues. One, all, or a combination of these were needed, along with a specific spell and a ritual for a Magician to work his or her magic. Indeed, a Magicians' wooden toolbox containing such items, and more was excavated in 1836.

Spells

Spells are chanted words. Words and spells were of upmost importance to the ancient Egyptians as they believed words, spoken and written (hieroglyphics), are a creative power influencing the supernatural energies to bring about the outcome asked for and create new realities. What you speak about comes about. They also used spells and mixtures of ingredients to cure illnesses and injuries.

Hieroglyphs

This was the writing system used by the ancient Egyptians, a symbolic picture instead of words. It was written by professional people due to the complexity, length of time and skill it took to understand and learn hieroglyphs. The simpler writing techniques known as hieratic and demotic were used for normal communication likes letters and other ordinary matters.

It was thought for a brief time only hieroglyphs would come to life, but it has long been thought hieroglyphics hold the 'secrets of the gods' and the deities' divine power was infused into the hieroglyph. Hieroglyphics (a permeant form of communication) are seen on the inside of tombs, monuments and temples. Spells using hieroglyphics were carved on the inside of pyramids after death to ensure the safe passage of the deceased to the afterlife. These were known as the Pyramid Texts. Later, after this became public knowledge, the Pyramid Texts became the Coffin Texts, and they can be seen carved extensively onto coffins.

AMULETS

An amulet is a small item carried or worn by a person to bring them protection, magic and good luck. In ancient Egypt the use of amulets was popular, most people wore them, and they were used for both the living and the dead. Amulets could be symbolic; *The Ankh* symbol for example, or they could be made to resemble a God or deity to initiate the spirit of the said deity.

Amulets could be necklaces, bracelets, rings or other items. Usually made of a quartz paste. Those of high-end quality would be made from turquoise, gold, serpentine or lapis lazuli amongst other substances.

For the deceased, the most popular amulet was one of The Eye of Horus and has been discovered in multiple excavations in Egypt. Perhaps though, the most important amulet used (particularly for the living) was one shaped as the scarab beetle.

Many amulets were carved in the shape of this creature. The top of the amulet would look like the scarab beetle, the underside would be flat with an inscription bearing the person's name, a God or symbol for example.

The scarab beetle was held in high esteem because in ancient Egypt the name 'scarab' also meant *kheper;* meaning 'to exist'. Therefore, a keeper of a scarab amulet would always exist, and so the scarab came to be a symbol of life. Further meaning was assigned to this creature as the scarab beetle (in nature) rolls dung balls into sunny bright places. This is hugely significant to the ancient Egyptians as it resembled the actions of their sun God, RA, when he rolled the sun across the skies every night. Finally, they also associated the scarab beetle with their God Atum, who had children without sexual intercourse. They believed scarab beetles did the same. This belief was proved wrong however... the scarab beetle (after mating) places her eggs in the dung (to provide food upon birth) and then rolls it as described earlier. The Egyptians just never saw scarabs mating and so assumed they didn't.

THE HOUSE OF LIFE (*PER ANKH*)

The House of Life, a building for the library of a temple, would store The Magicians knowledge and is where they were schooled and trained in this important work. The knowledge learnt was written on papyri (material made from a water plant to write or paint on) and were hidden in the walls of the temples and kept in private sections to maintain secrecy.

These writings became books (a collection of papyri) on magic. The Magicians were further entrusted with these secrets and books to prevent them from falling into the hands of individuals. Titles of these books included: The Book of Knowledge of Secrets of the

Laboratory, Spells for Warding off the Evil Eye and The Book of Magical Protection of the King in His Palace.

The Magicians also consulted in The House of Life with individuals who came to see them with their problem or query. It is here The Magicians would provide dream interpretations, make potions, provide amulets, perform healings and spells or aid in counteracting bad influences plus many other magical duties.

The Temple of Eduf on the west bank of The Nile River is one of the most important Houses of Life and can still be visited today. Copies of spells have been recovered from Eduf and other Houses of Life.

It's interesting to note ancient Egyptians would have a secret name (the *ren*). Their belief in spells was so strong they would never use their real name in case an un-pure spell or their removal from history was used upon it. If the un-pure spell was cast on their common name, not their real name, it wouldn't work. It is said only the individual and the Gods knew their real name as if their secret name was discovered, power could be gained over them.

Examples and recoveries of all the aforementioned are located in many of the museums around the world as well as in Egypt itself.

As previously mentioned, words and spells were extremely important and significant to the ancient Egyptians. Let's consider are own schooling and schools of today. It is still called *spelling* or *learning to spell*, and it is called *spelling* for a reason.

Maybe we all have been misled of the words' actual power and meaning, with the real truth of *spelling* <u>and therefore the power we hold for ourselves,</u> conveniently emitted and hidden from society...

Like most of ancient Egyptian culture, Egyptian magic

is incredibly detailed and complex and its only possible to give you but a slither of it here, but I do hope it intrigues you to discover more.

Perhaps you can make a Book of Magic of your own from your own secret knowledge of life. How cool would it be to have it passed down through all your future generations? Because–we are–after all, all Magicians.

Raise a wand to this new magical season upon us.

The next telegram will arrive on 11th May 2021.

The Moon Telegram

Date: May 11th, 2021,
England

Hello to one and all,

I wanted to send a telegram this month about energy fields, of which all living things emit. You may have noticed we cannot always control the collective vibe and that of others, yet their energy fields affect us, if we let it. We can though, govern and protect our own energy centre and field. We can become aware of how paramount it is to understand our energy field and how this affects us individually and in turn, our lives.

Everything has a frequency (a vibration) which is emitted outwards from a central core. From emotions to thoughts to all cells. As humans we can control our frequencies of our energy field because we have the ability to choose, we are the only form of nature with this ability, making humans the highest form of all living things. That in itself is a magnificent privilege.

If we look at nature, everything has a core at its centre. There is a 'core' from which it grows as a youngster or seedling and its individual energy radiates out from that place. For example, cut tomatoes, oranges, peppers, apples or a cabbage in half and you will find a core where it's personal coding sits and radiates out from – in frequencies. These frequencies, even of fruits and vegetables, can be recorded by a machine and its frequency recorded and translated into its equivalent sound frequency, so we as humans can hear it. The music a pineapple emits is simply stunning and so happy! Proof that any living 'thing' is more than its visible self, and humans are no different. These machines can be purchased from reputable companies or search YouTube to watch videos of the music fruits and vegetables emit.

We also radiate our energy out from our core centre and this cloud of beaming energy (mostly) unseen to the eye, un-smelt by the nose and untouchable by the hand is real and extends far beyond the body we think of as 'us' as a person.

THE HUMAN HEART

The human heart is the main organ keeping us alive but is also far more than this. It is our source of life and associated with love, dreams and our purpose. Like the vegetables with their individual coding, we too have this placed in our central energy core. The creator of humans, however, wanted to make sure our coding, destiny, fate, love, purpose, whichever word works you, existed and stood every chance of becoming. That you stood every chance of living out your destiny. Interestingly, the heart is the only organ not effected by the disease cancer, (studies in America are continuing on this) why do you think that is? So, we can stay alive as long as possible to live out our destiny. To be our best selves and enjoy life to the fullest and fulfil our reason for being here.

This is why it is so important to listen to what's in your 'heart'. Are you?

The frequency of love (also known as the miracle tone) registers at 528Hz and is where love, miracles, transformation exist. The 528 Hz frequency is often used in music, guided mediations and other audible productions to help us attune us to this transformational, beautiful, natural and healing energy. 528Hz is also the frequency within the solar plexus, our core of our being. If you are in anger, for example, this emotion registers at around 150 Hz can you see how you are mismatch? Raise your frequency if you want to attract the higher things of life, good health and that of *your heart.*

... back to energy fields at large.

The invisible energy field humans emit extends six to ten feet in front of us, behind us, to our left side, the right side, above and below. This is actually a large area; we take up far more space than we think. If we are around others, it can be tricky to define where we end and the other person begins. Think of being in a car, a plane, the tube and all those individual energies mixing.

We can often tell the vibe of someone before they even speak because, whether we realise it or not, we read their core energy first then listen to words. It's worth remembering once more - energy doesn't lie; words can. It would be prudent to trust feelings and energy over words.

This energy field is one reason we pick up on others' personalities and intentions, but also how we can feel drained and sapped. We've stood too close or for too long with a negative energy or toxic person and they have drained or fed from your field. We can take on the emotions of that person... ever met someone feeling happy and fine and then left feeling moody? Their emotions leaked into our field. Got on the bus feeling excited and left feeling upset? It's likely the person sat in the seat before was sad and we have absorbed it.

Be sure your feelings and emotions are actually yours

and not those of another person's and protect your own energy fiercely!

Here are a few tips -

- Stand a least six feet away from a person you find difficult, draining or negative or, place as much of a gap as you can between you both.
- If your mood has suddenly changed say to yourself or out loud 'Remove anything that it is not mine'.
- Zip up - before entering a situation or being around tricky people, imagine yourself cocooned in a black sleeping bag or woollen coat (it covers your whole head and feet too) and say to yourself 'zip up' and see the coat or sleeping bag being zipped up. This stops our energy leaking out and others encroaching on it.
- Before leaving the house imagine a bright white bubble around yourself which stays with you all day. An alternative to zipping up because who wants to take on the energies of the entirety of society!
- Stay away from shopping malls and busy places if you are super empathic (i.e., absorb other people's emotions).
- Take a shower or rinse your arms in cold water to rinse off energy.
- Shake your body, flick your arms and legs out. Stamp your feet or clap your hands to send 'it' away in order to alter your state.
- Ground. Everyday ground yourself. This helps to keep you calmer, centred and clearer. There are many ways to ground yourself.
  Popular ones include: walking or standing barefoot on soil, sand or grass (any type of earth) for ten minutes, going outside in nature or fresh air, sitting

or being around water or trees, mediating, breathing deeply (the power of breath is phenomenal), smell something of nature like flowers or a natural scent which feels good to you when you smell it, placing your hands or feet in water.

AURAS

Auras are *this* energy field seen with the human eye. It's like a glow around the human body. It moves like smoke, around, up and down the surface of the body about an inch wide and can be various colours. The colours, amongst other symbolic meanings, often correspond with the individual chakras. For example, if someone has a blue aura this can be related to the throat chakra which reflects communication, speaking, voice, self-expression, creativity. Entertainers of all kinds and artists frequently have blue auras as they are essentially communicators through their work.

The colours can change, as can their intensity, and everyone has the ability to see their own aura as well as that of others, I will tell you how shortly. Everyone can see an aura with practice, but some find it easier than others. Those who are more clairvoyant (clear seeing) definitely find this easier. You can refresh yourselves on this skill by re-reading the January telegram.

Much has been written on auras and its worth researching more and practicing the skill if it interests you. There's nothing quite like it when you witness the colourful smoky energy around the body. It makes one understand how our thoughts, feelings and emotions are transmitted from us without words. Experienced aura readers can tell you a lot about yourself just from viewing your aura.

Chakra colours for reference. Their meanings can be more deeply explored if you feel called to.

- Root chakra. Colour: Red
- Sacral chakra. Colour: Orange
- Solar plexus chakra. Colour: Yellow
- Heart chakra. Colour: Green
- Throat chakra. Colour: Blue
- Third-eye chakra. Colour: Indigo/purple
- Crown chakra. Colour: Purple/violet, can be a purplish white

HOW TO SEE YOUR OWN AURA

- Be in a quiet darkened room. Night-time is best so there is little, or no light is creeping in from behind the curtains.
- Stand in front of a mirror.
- Stare just above your head and hold the gaze or stare just behind your shoulder and hold the gaze. Look past the body or head, not directly at it.
- After a time and with practice, you will see glimpses or all of your aura.

HOW TO SEE SOMEONE ELSE'S AURA

- Again, stand in a quiet dark room.
- Have the person whose aura you want to see, or read, stand against a white or light-coloured wall. Stare just above their head and hold the gaze or stare just behind their shoulder and hold the gaze. Look past the body or head, not directly at it. After a time and with practice you will see glimpses or all of their aura.

Wishing you success in seeing your aura and living from the heart. What colour do you think your aura will be? And what colour actually is it? It might well show a difference between what you think or believe your core energy is and what it actually is, offering one personal insights.

The next telegram will arrive 10th June 2021.

The Moon Telegram

Date: 10ᵗʰ June, 2021
England

Hello to one and all,

I wanted to bring you a topic this month which you can use and bring into your everyday life to receive answers, protection and guidance from your personalised supernatural team–AKA–your Higher Self and your Spirit Guides. Plus, a bonus technique for receiving answers or inspired solutions known as the Key Drop Power Nap.

The Key Drop Power Nap has been used for decades and decades by some of our most brilliant geniuses, like Einstein and Aristotle.

But first. Your Higher Self and Spirit Guides.

Every person has a Higher Self and Spirit Guides, whether they are aware of this or not (most aren't). Some call their Spirit Guides guardian angels; the title is irrelevant, although Angels are a different and separate entity all together.

Spirit Guides are assigned to us and they reside in the higher frequencies of the Cosmos. You can tap into to them and call on them in the same way you would a friend or mentor on earth. If you have been practicing your supernatural guidance techniques from January's telegram you will find this easier as this is how they also communicate.

Our Higher Self

Our Higher Self is the unseen part of us also residing in the higher frequencies of the Cosmos.

When we came to earth, via our parents, a part of us remained in those mysterious realms of the Cosmos. Our Higher Self is the part of us that is of the same as the creator of the Universe or Cosmos.

The term you give to your creator doesn't matter, it is all the same.

The Higher Self is our guiding mother ship; wise, loving, encouraging and all-knowing leading us forward always. It is an anchor to which we are rooted to and always connected to by an energy.

You can become closer and converse more with your Higher Self, not only in meditation although this is perhaps one of the keyways, but by being in touch with your heart, being at peace, spending time in nature, tuning into your intuition more and knowing the power of the words you speak... the effect of the words you choose to speak. As per the April telegram it is called *spelling* or *learning to spell* for a reason and your words have mystical powers. Any or all of these methods will close the gap between you and Higher Self and will help fill the inner void one may feel.

Spirit Guides (Guides)

As well as our permanent, beautiful and powerful Higher Self, we all have Spirit Guides as well. What a team or advisory board we have in the unseen! Often, we forget this and underutilise them massively. We forget to ask for help, for answers, for ideas and for miracles.

It is thought we have three to four Guides at any one

time and each of these Guides plays a different role or purpose in our individual lives. One may help with protection, one may help with family, another might be there to help craft your skills or be your supernatural PR agent. Ever noticed how others got their break, the next step up or an opportunity by a random meeting of someone, a spontaneous idea, taking an inspired action or off the back of a disguised mishap? Most times this is the case. I guarantee, however it occurred, that the situation or circumstances surrounding it could not have been orchestrated purely on their own merits.

Guides often change over time as our needs or situations change. When this happens there is almost like a changing of the guards as older ones leave and the new Guides come in, who have different or more relevant experience, knowledge and wisdom that we need at the said period of our life.

WHO ARE OUR SPIRIT GUIDES?

Spirit Guides can be loved ones who have transitioned from here on earth back into the energies of the Cosmos at large but usually we don't know our guides personally. They can be anyone from the beginning of time, any country, any culture or race. Ancestors can also be guides, and it's worth mentioning that even if your ancestors are not one of your guides, you can still call on them. I believe it prudent to never forget our ancestors and thank them. It's because of them we are here today. They are full of love, wisdom, and guidance they are eager to impart on us.

You may not always know the name of your Guides; it doesn't matter if you don't. If you do want to find out the name of your main Guide, ask them! If you want to try, set the intention (same as asking) before falling asleep at bedtime for your main Guide to let you know their name as you dream. You may well remember it in the morning, hear it upon waking or a name may stick out to you later in the day.

What do our Spirit Guides do?

Each Spirit Guide plays a role: protection, guidance and inspiration to mention some. They are assigned specifically to us and you trust they deeply understand us and our situations. They work as part of the unseen forces assisting you, many times you have been protected from danger or a situation you're not even aware of. Example, because you were 'inspired' to grab a coffee on the way to work you avoided a car accident, or you felt guided to visit a museum or place of interest and met the love of your life. Take inventory of your life so far and you will see how this has played out. You do of course have free will and do not need to listen to any of it, but it sure makes life easier and smoother, and more fun, if you do.

I want to round up June's telegram by letting you know of the Key Drop Power Nap in order to receive an inspired idea, a creative solution or 'right' answer from the unseen forces of the Cosmos. For some it is more fitting than meditation... meditation is powerful but it's not the only way.

Many creative types use this method when they feel blocked or stuck. As I mentioned at the beginning The Key Drop Power Nap is not new, but few are in the know of this powerful technique. Here's how it works and how you do it.

- You need a key or a metal object and a ceramic plate.
- Raise your question. You can do this by setting the

intention for an answer for it, by asking your question out loud, asking it in your head or by writing the question down. You only need to ask or state once, not a thousand times. Nor do your words need to be perfect. The Universe and supernatural realms understand your feelings, emotions and imagination. Therefore, your question and desire for an answer or solution needs to genuine and authentic.
- Sit in a comfy chair, lie on your bed, the sofa or wherever you want to take a nap.
- Hold the key in your palm. Extend your arm out and angle your hand over the plate. The plate needs to be on the floor directly under in your hand holding the key.
- Drift off for a sneaky nap.
- As you reach the deeper sleep levels and lose consciousness, the key or metal object will drop from your palm onto the plate awakening you by the clatter it causes.
- It is in this awaking state of sleep (called hypnogogic) you allow connection to the unseen forces, your guides also, and the mired of other supernatural creative help available that in normal wake state you don't have access to.
- The idea, solution or answer will come to you.
- You will hear it, see it as an image or vision, feel it or realise the answer.
- It's best to write it down as these can slip away as quick as they arrived, and you don't always remember.
- The answer or thought may not be familiar, logical or it might seem odd but there will be something in it if you follow it or pay attention to it.
- As with anything practice gives you mastery.

I truly hope you learn and utilise all the help and support you have; it brings great comfort and assistance. Everyone is different and each will ask and receive in different ways. You know when you've hit the right way or the right answer because it feels like relief.

Truth feels like relief.

This concludes Volume One of The Moon Telegrams.

Thank you for reading

Hopefully you enjoyed the first volume of The Moon Telegrams. If you would like to leave a review it would be much appreciated. I love to hear your comments or requests for future topics. It also helps more people discover these publications.

Volume Two of The Moon Telegrams (July 2021-December 2021) will be released in December 2021.

Sign up to my newsletter and community. You will receive all upcoming information on my latest books, aspects of my author life, behind the scenes, meet ups, exclusive and exciting news. I look forward to having you in my community!

https://www.annaliesemorgan.com/newsletter

Contact Annaliese Morgan

Write to me at my London Office:
Annaliese Morgan
49 Greek Street
London
W1D 4EG

E-Mail me: hello@annaliesemorgan.com

Visit me on social media or go to my website:
annaliesemorgan.com
Instagram: @annaliese.morgan
facebook.com/annaliesehmorgan

Bibliography

Alexander, Skye. Mermaids: The Myths, Legends and Lore. (Massachusetts: Adam Media, 2012)

Ancient Symbols *(www.ancient-symbols.com)*

Brier, Bob. Ancient Egyptian Magic: Spells, Incantations, Potions, Stories, and Rituals. (New York: Quill, 1980)

Connolly Cove *(https://www.connollycove.com)*

Druidry *(https://druidry.org)*

Fictional Creatures *(www.fictionalcreatures.com)*

Learn Religions *(www.learnreligions.com)*

Live Science *(www.livescience.com)*

Mythology *(https://mythology.net)*

One Tree Planted *(www.onetreeplanted.org)*

Robbins, Tony Ted Talks

Ronnberg, Amy (Editor-in-chief). The Book of Symbols: Reflections on Archetypal Images. (Koln: Taschen, 2010)

Royal Museum Greenwich *(www.rmg.co.uk)*

Scotsclan *(https://www.scotclans.com)*

Supreme Council of Antiquities *(http://www.sca-egypt.org/eng/SITE_Edfu.html)*

Tree Council *(https://www.treecouncil.ie)*

World History Encyclopaedia *(www.worldhistory.org)*

You Are Creators *(https://www.youtube.com/watch?v=2up6M5h8NYo&t=28s)*

www.ingramcontent.com/pod-product-compliance
Lightning Source LLC
Chambersburg PA
CBHW021159080526
44588CB00008B/416